# We're from Kenya

Emma Lynch

Heinemann
LIBRARY

Young Explorer

**www.heinemann.co.uk/library**
Visit our website to find out more information about **Heinemann Library** books.

To order:
☎ Phone 44 (0) 1865 888066
🗎 Send a fax to 44 (0) 1865 314091
💻 Visit the Heinemann Bookshop at www.heinemann.co.uk/library to browse our catalogue and order online.

First published in Great Britain by Heinemann Library, Halley Court, Jordan Hill, Oxford OX2 8EJ, part of Harcourt Education.
Heinemann is a registered trademark of Harcourt Education Ltd.

Editorial: Jilly Attwood and Kate Bellamy
Design: Ron Kamen and Celia Jones
Illustrations: Darren Lingard
Picture Research: Maria Joannou and Erica Newbery
Production: Severine Ribierre

Originated by Ambassador Litho Ltd

Printed and bound in China by South China Printing Company

ISBN 0 431 11948 1
09 08 07 06 05
10 9 8 7 6 5 4 3 2 1

British Library Cataloguing in Publication Data

Lynch, Emma
  We're From Kenya
  967.6'2043

A full catalogue record for this book is available from the British Library.

Acknowledgements
The publishers would like to thank the following for permission to reproduce photographs: Audrius Tomonis p. **30c**; Corbis p. **30a**; Harcourt Education pp. **5a, 5b, 6a, 6b, 7a, 7b, 8a, 8b, 9a, 9b, 10a, 10b, 11a, 11b, 12a, 12b, 13a, 13b, 14, 15a, 15b, 16a, 16b, 17a, 17b, 18a, 18b, 19a, 19b, 20a, 20b, 21, 22, 23a, 23b, 24a, 24b, 25a, 25b, 26a, 26b, 27a, 27b, 28a, 28b, 29a, 29b, 30b** (Roy Maconachie/EASI-Images).

Cover photograph of Grace and her school friends, reproduced with permission of Harcourt Education/Roy Maconachie/EASI-Images.

Our thanks to Chris Waldron for his assistance in the preparation of this book.

Every effort has been made to contact copyright holders of any material reproduced in this book. Any omissions will be rectified in subsequent printings if notice is given to the publishers.

The paper used to print this book comes from sustainable resources.

# Contents

Words appearing in the text in bold, **like this**, are explained in the Glossary.

 Find out more about Kenya at
www.heinemannexplore.co.uk

# Where is Kenya?

To learn more about Kenya we meet three children who live there. Kenya is a country in Africa. Kenya has the second highest mountain in Africa, Mount Kenya.

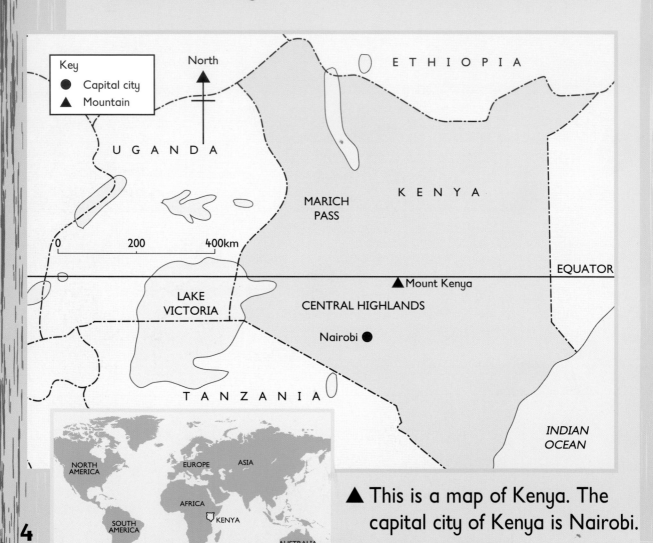

**Key**
- ● Capital city
- ▲ Mountain

North

ETHIOPIA

UGANDA

KENYA

MARICH
PASS

0    200    400km

EQUATOR

▲ Mount Kenya

LAKE
VICTORIA

CENTRAL HIGHLANDS

Nairobi ●

TANZANIA

INDIAN
OCEAN

NORTH
AMERICA

EUROPE    ASIA

AFRICA

SOUTH
AMERICA    KENYA

AUSTRALIA

▲ This is a map of Kenya. The capital city of Kenya is Nairobi.

Kenya has low land near the sea. The weather here is **tropical**. Kenya has high land in the centre of the country. It is very dry in the high land.

Kenya has some large cities but it has a lot of countryside too. ▶

# Meet Ronnie

Ronnie is eight years old. He lives in a house in Nairobi. Ronnie lives in a house with his mother, father, and baby sister Connie.

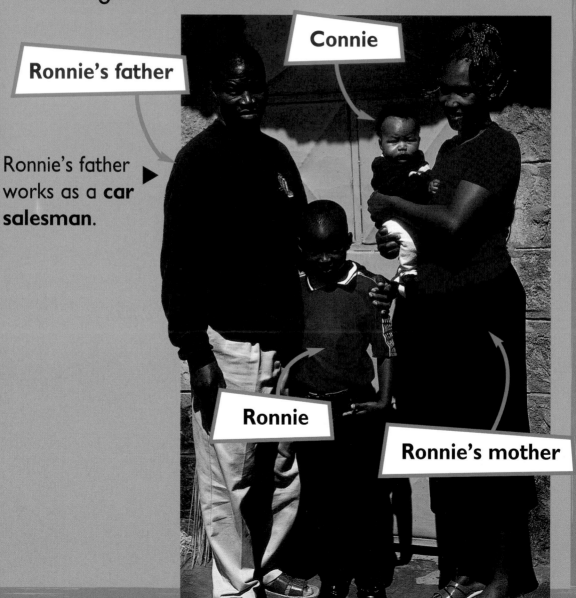

Connie

Ronnie's father

Ronnie's father works as a **car salesman**.

Ronnie

Ronnie's mother

▲ Ronnie's family eat breakfast
together every morning.

Ronnie's mother stays at home to look
after Connie. Ronnie helps his mother
at home. He keeps his room tidy and
he helps look after Connie.

# Ronnie's school

Ronnie goes to school five days a week. He learns maths, English, art, **Swahili**, citizenship, religious education and **environmental** studies. He likes art best.

▲ There are 35 children in Ronnie's class. They have their lessons in Swahili.

At lunch time, Ronnie and his friends play in the playground. There are swings and a climbing frame. They can play football too.

Ronnie's class eat their ▶ lunch in the classroom.

9

# Play time

After school Ronnie has to do an hour of homework. Then he likes to play. Ronnie enjoys reading, drawing and watching television. He likes to ride his bike too.

◀ Ronnie and his friends play outside on the street.

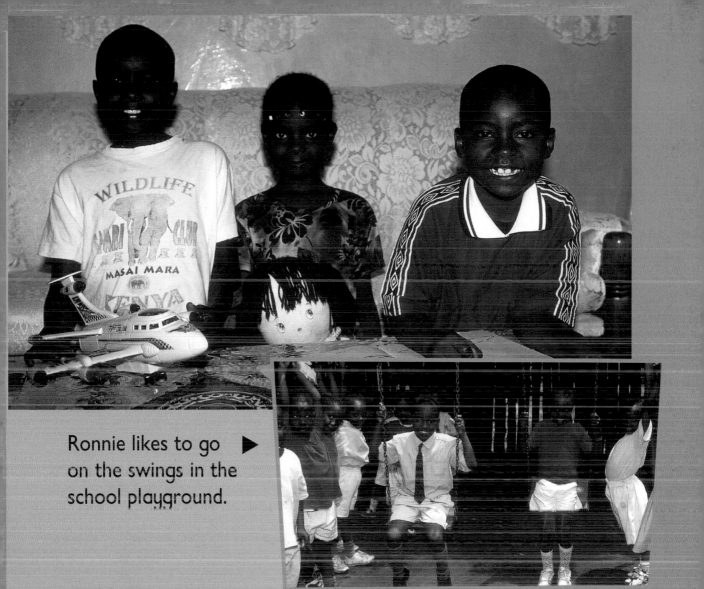

Ronnie likes to go ▶
on the swings in the
school playground.

Ronnie's best friends are Lillian
and Joseph. They play together at
home and at school. They like
playing at school because there
is a big playground.

# Farming and fishing

Kenya has a lot of different farms. The high land in the centre of Kenya is good for growing plants. Tea and coffee are grown in Kenya and sold all over the world.

Many people grow and ▶ pick tea in Kenya.

fish

Some people grow fruit, vegetables and rice to sell at the markets. Some people grow flowers to sell. Fishermen work on Lake Victoria and sell the fish they catch.

# Meet Grace

Grace is seven years old. She lives in Mwea, a small village in the middle of Kenya. Grace lives with her mother, father, brother and two sisters.

▼ Everyone in Mwea knows each other.

Grace's mother

Grace's father

Grace

Grace's brother

Grace's sisters

▲ Grace has lots of space to play outside. She likes skipping.

Grace's house has no water or **electricity**. Her family get water from a stream. They use wood to make a fire for cooking food on.

# Grace's work

Grace goes to school for five days a week. She likes going to school because she has lots of friends there. When she grows up, Grace wants to be a teacher.

Grace and her ▶ friends work hard at school.

After school, Grace does her homework. Then she helps her parents. She collects firewood for cooking with and water from the stream.

Grace's main job ▶ is to look after the goats.

# Food

Grace's parents are farmers. They grow rice to eat and to sell at the market in Mwea. With the money they make at market, they buy cabbages, potatoes or tomatoes.

Most farming in Kenya is done by hand. ▶

For a special treat, Grace's parents buy beef to eat. Grace's favourite food is rice and beans, but she likes it best with beef!

Grace likes to help her mother sort beans for cooking. ▶

# Market day

Markets are very important in Kenya. People go to markets to buy and sell food and clothes.

Market day is always very busy. ▶

▲ In some places, people dress in **traditional** clothes or jewellery for market day.

People also go to the market to meet their friends and talk. Most Kenyans buy their clothes from clothes markets.

# Meet Betty and Naomi

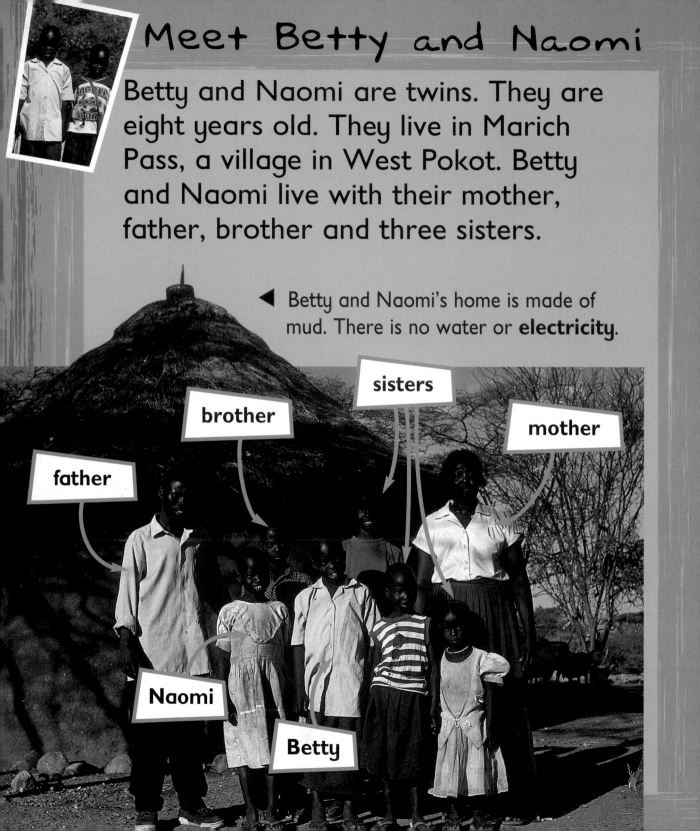

Betty and Naomi are twins. They are eight years old. They live in Marich Pass, a village in West Pokot. Betty and Naomi live with their mother, father, brother and three sisters.

◀ Betty and Naomi's home is made of mud. There is no water or **electricity**.

sisters

brother

mother

father

Naomi

Betty

▲ West Pokot often has **droughts**.

West Pokot is very dry. The family get water from the river. Sometimes there is not enough rain for them to grow food. They have to rely on **charities** to bring them food.

# At school

Betty and Naomi go to school five days a week. In Kenya, Primary School is free but Secondary School is not. The family will have to sell some goats to pay for the twins to go to Secondary School.

Betty and Naomi live close to school so they can walk there. ▶

At school, the children sit on the floor for lessons because there are no desks. Betty and Naomi learn English, **Swahili**, maths, history, science and art. They like maths best.

◀ At break time the children like to play football or basketball.

# Work

After school the twins do their homework. They have jobs to do at home too. They care for the goats and collect firewood. They help to cook and clean.

▼ Betty and Naomi help to carry water from the river twice a day.

Betty and Naomi's ▶
mother runs the
local shop.

Betty and Naomi help look after their
little sister because their parents
work. Their father teaches at the
nursery school. He also shows
**tourists** around the area.

# Tourism

Tourists come to Kenya to see its beautiful mountains and beaches. Lots of people in Kenya work by helping **tourists**. They show tourists around, work as drivers or work in hotels.

◀ There are lots of large hotels in Kenya for tourists to stay in.

▼ Tourists on a safari can see animals living in the wild.

Lots of tourists come to Kenya to see the animals that live there. They go on a **safari**. They can see lions, elephants, zebras, hippos and leopards.

# Kenyan fact file

**Flag**       **Capital city**      **Money**

**Nairobi**

**Kenyan shilling**

## Religion
• Most people in Kenya are Christians. There are some Muslims too.

## Language
• English and **Swahili** are the official languages of Kenya. There are many tribal languages too.

### Try speaking Swahili!
Jambo! ........................................... Hello!
Hujambo?...................................... How are you?
Asante ........................................... Thank you.

 Find out more about Kenya at
www.heinemannexplore.co.uk

# Glossary

**car salesman** someone who works by selling cars

**charity** group that helps people who are poor or in need

**drought** dry weather and no rain for a long time

**electricity** power used for heating, lighting and to work machines

**environment** the natural world in which people plants and animals live

**safari** journey to see wild animals

**Swahili** official language of Kenya

**tourist** someone who is visiting on holiday

**tradition** something that has been going for a very long time without changing

**tropical** hot and muggy, with lots of rain

## More books to read

*Around the World: Clothes*, Margaret Hall (Heinemann Library, 2002)

*Continents: Africa*, Leila Foster (Heinemann Library, 2002)

*Letters from around the World: Kenya*, Ali Brownlie (Cherrytree Books, 2002)

*We Come From: Kenya*, Wambui Kairi (Hodder Wayland, 2002)

# Index